Chasing Skirt

A book of poetry & prose

Words of Praise for Chasing Skirt:

The Sweet Pinkham

"These words are a truth and an anthem of why he chases and why he loves the women he does. Fantastic Delight!."

Azure

"Chasing Skirt is even better than his first book, richer and more livelier in its depth and wonder. The modern phasing is so dynamic in its borderline new divinity that we are compelled to see this world in such gritty modern terms that we can only love the experience of it."

The Danger

"Wicked Cool! The juxtaposition of words and phrases in Chasing Skirt rival no other and truly speak to a new voice in modern punk literature. "

This book is dedicated to the beautiful pursuit, a dance best played out with the intentions of exploration and wonderment for a delicious woman in whom you can love, even if for a brief moment.

for the lads . rose city 'til i die!

Copyright of Sunshine Ink, 2010.
Portland

ISBN: 9780976856016

Chasing Skirt and the poems and prose contained therein are the copyright of Sunshine Ink and lucas klesch. All rights reserved.

Chasing Skirt poetry & prose

Saturation Skin to Skin Reprise
Mystic Temp
Next Stop Wonderland
Plumes of Pleasure
The Prettiest Pussy in Portland
The Joy and Sunshine of No-Thing
Oh Virginia
Late Night Melody
The Cost of Entropy
All About the Betties
Retro Punk Virginia
The Artist Samurai
Conduction
Nostalgia is Ink
Sounds of Video Crack
untitled strands
Strange Sex Act Painting
The Finite Infinity
Wicked Delicious
An Infamous Return to Bohemian Artistry
Magic Nostalgia
A Smash & Grab Affair
My Vibe is Jazz
The Song of You
Short Steps of Babble
Red, Gold and Blonde
Universal Vibrational Energy
Inherent Mania
Jean-Claude's Truffles
Hop Scotch Canvas
Catch and Release Theory

Everyone Needs a Bohemian
Barfly's Words and Sex
Futbol Politicos
Just Words
The # 44 line to the Village
Punk Dating
Best in Show
Perfection
Flapper Roots
dirty old man
i like Parades
Inked Barstools
Skin Season is not Boot Season
Flames are Blue
Per Capita Skin
whores hats and painted skin
This Show is Inked
Punk's Guide to Dating
drinking, smoking, cursing delicious barfly
Be a Character
Naked Betties
ala carte
Delicious Luminous Doll
la la OC
Slim Sexy
Prolific Ecstatic Joy
Verbose Projections
Entropy Kisses
on that note

Saturation Skin to Skin Reprise

will you dance with me she asked
as we pass in the hall
her erotic scent grabs my sensual antennas
i can taste her pheromones on my tongue
delicious anticipation of
                    saturation skin to skin
you make my kitty purr she whispered in my ear
the scent of flirtatious words fill the small space
between us   the heat is so generous
her warmth is a sultry magnet
a delicious compass that leads to
              saturation skin to skin
I am hot as hell today she said
as she threw herself on the velvet couch
the pink puma glistening
as she slowly pulled her skirt up
              a delicious smile
    craving lust in her eyes
beautiful green to swim my way
            to saturation skin to skin
you are so naughty she whispered in my ear
as I leaned down to kiss her cheek
she led my hand to her inner thigh
her puma juices dripped from anticipation
of pleasure I created in her mind
            saturation skin to skin

I want you to read me that poem again
it's like tantric nudges that lead
to pure delicious delight
            after dinner cosmos

that keep you winking for the opportunity
    to lick your lips
        moan and wail
            saturation skin to skin
I had flashbacks to your sexiness she whispered
as if you were beside me
        a frame of red lights in dark rooms
drink smoking sultry tunes
all the anticipation you bring
            saturation skin to skin
    I want to feel again
how intensely you make me spasm
my muscles clenched in ecstasy
scrumptious orgasms
            saturation skin to skin
hours later I could still smell her on me
that perfume of debauchery
is saturation skin to skin

Mystic Temp

she was a mind reading stenographer
          back in the day
when they were called psychic

Next Stop Wonderland

the times always dictates a mirrored view
parlayed with broken mixes of tyvek sliding doors
captured on Polaroids left on the T (train)
                     next stop wonderland
Back Bay, Copley Square
Boston is just like L.A. and the Rose City
its where I met Bukowski at the Bitter End
Dylan in the alleys   -   its all just a parade
of different characters to entertain
like metropolitan ice cream on a hot summers day
the sticky wet humidity
        sends lovers out at night
to revel in passion
I see them, meet them, on lucid streets
dripping neon colors   seductive light
as strident charges linger to the pace of fools' voices
we all listen to vibrant noises in the dark
love is sex in a hot sticky environment
when it remembers the anti-climactic noise made
during nights of forlorn adventures
I am a climactic world – wind of thoughts
racing racing racing ever faster
          towards long waking nights
          of sleep to wake again
all those colors the rose city brings
   to trust   sex and junkies go together

Plumes of Pleasure

joy is a penchant for success
when mania junkies find the lion laying in bed naked
his words and touches
    are silk on the skin
soft and sensual after you disrobe
    for a night of pleasure
  lay me down on these golden sheets
as I send careening plumes of pleasure
    chakras filled with the energy of a lion
as night flows into day
    naked bodies lay strewn on damp sheets
sticky silk skin jazzed
        by the night's endeavors

The Prettiest Pussy in Portland

a sultry blend of classical beauty
elegantly wicked
i only throw ones when the clothes come off
sometimes a primer gets it going
the wink and smile   then rapport
she asks what I like
moving in closer   hand on the thigh
its designed to draw attention to her sexpot
the beauty of the magic garden is to know when to bite
she then introduced me to the prettiest pussy in Portland   with a sure smile of enticement
I said it is and off she slithered to twirl the stage
a pause   wink   from the mirror
the cherry on my fag is glowing red in the dim light of the garden   half a pint of pabst
                              a smile or two
i have the prettiest pussy in portland
such a delicious delight
                    her two perfect erect nipples   I pause on the inhale to gaze upon luscious lips
                    sultry jazz roars from the
I can hear the video poker bells
a man talking to the hot little bartender   -   I smile wink at her as she probes
                    the prettiest pussy in portland
a deep inhale and I can smell her lust for me
an alluring combo of dancing for lecherous men
       the comfort strangers bring
she brushes her finger on my cheek

                    to tell me i am cute   i
take a big gulp of my beer
suck on my fag multiple times
   she is directly across from me
gazing at me with a smile
as she bends over showing him
                the prettiest pussy in portland
my grin an enticement to her
        i could see the lust in her eyes
the allure of her body 'til the music stopped
my fag was done so i stomped it out
finished my beer   watched another doll
and waited 'til it was time
for the prettiest pussy in Portland
                to seduce me again

The Joy and Sunshine of No-Thing

jib jib jive marches the ideas of no-thing
when last we met joy and sunshine
they were lost upon a golden road of snowy delight
two bums lost in Dharma
it is no-thing which leads them asunder
42 which leads them under – and – over
we go 'til the golden road is grey no more
              azure is joy
    i am sunshine
  this is the mantra of no-thing
devotees lead to unlimited devotion in Dharma bums of
Beatnik proportions
    where Kerouac drank wine
            until he preserved his words
the words sang beat songs
of smoking jazz bars from Harlem to Frisco
    the nocturnal tune of sweet saxophones
ethereal bohemians swaying
all around joy and sunshine
the Dharma beat
            at once frenetic in its chaotic vibe
as the strings pluck themselves ever faster
down low the pitch goes
      the melody is a blue note of azure
          he is joy
            i am sunshine
together we gather bums of harmonic design
smoking tea in a dark Harlem night
miles away the speed of hepcats swing
in the fold of infinity where there is no respite
this ever changing mental chaos

propels soft streams of miles from blue
hidden in the denizens of Harlem as we sing the heroin
blues   late into the night
     so long my friend   for
     azure is joy
          i am sunshine
long past midnight we have gone
as one more joint winks at us
the ladies have passed us by
we find the darkest minutes in the night
soon the blues brings us around
the sun rises on Dharma bums

Oh Virginia

free flowing verse sitting on a Virginia stool
in a cafe bar as old as the culture of the city
manic and rose is Virginia
who celebrates the punk in me
alternative to the mainstream
inked rockabilly dolls   cool hepcats
smoking and drinking the day away

Late Night Melody

this night is like soft brush strokes on the edge
of a drum as Charlie plays a melancholy tune
i am just one lonely kat amidst this heartfelt world
    jazz musicians
feel their way through my thoughts
kick the tempo up a notch
as i ride ethereal streams
in this smoke filled room
back down goes the flow
i gaze across the bar
    to see one sole lady loving on me

The Cost of Entropy

deleted financials are the results of fun and mania
when control is left to a whim
the whim is fantastically evasive

i speak this as a means to control
   which as we all know costs entropy

honeys and the like   an evening of drink, drugs
         the potential of sex
  is the ignition of mania where chasing skirt
is the name of the   game
catch and release the preferred methodology
   so i can shag a new doll tomorrow
they declare it their act of womanizing
the antics of an appreciative devotee
of women who love to pleasure the sacred
an artist is emotional
     the ultimate gift of companionship
  the pleasure we all know
it is not always sexual but it is always intimate
   energy is the currency of both

All About the Betties

buffalo in the gap for dollar Pabst
   dapper kats   dolls
once played gentlemen sports
on green fields next to joyous kegs
highlighted in luscious demeanor
with cigarettes that smoke themselves
as the men drink cocktails   women red wine
elegant dolls scream dirty and loud
                    just like hipsters do
when the sacred O rains down on them
from my pulsing motion on vanilla sheets
opened by touch and whispered upon

Retro Punk Virginia

tiny retro curves in the punk inked style
  one last lunch with Virginia
over greasy burgers and dark pints of beer
    it's vintage here with orange glow globes
      scratched mahogany panels
the photography is black and white
        from the roaring twenties
  when my flapper girls
gave a roaring night to any accommodating kat
  it's almost time to say goodnight
  my sweet Virginia
if we could extend our stay just a few more days
  we could have a little fun
one more lunch to remember it all

The Artist Samurai

late nights talking to crazy dolls
is the modus of the rebel rousing doctrine
    it leaves you tired and mentally drained
such is the way of the artist samurai
  who juggles women like balls
orchestrating multiple conversations meetings
just to have one in the hand
              when the need arises
creativity is an ebb and flow of energy
the exaggerated desire to explore the female body
    creatively evoking pleasure
broken dolls just want to love
be loved in Marilyn's style
she mistook abuse adoration for love
  optimism is not the same as idealism
nor can you find it relaxing romanticism
    optimism is grounded in reality
knowing one can achieve the possibility
  idealism and romanticism are the land of magical
outcomes that occur preordained
  magic is the soul in pain that still needs to hope
        existence is possible
yet belief does not materialize
  the pain burrows deeper and deeper away
from the comfort of strangers
    where sunshine is our friend
    this pedestal i sit upon
it is going to hurt when i fall
  you cannot feel the trace scent
              i know is lost
when lives go in separate directions

the comfort of strangers are welcome places
to seek respite from the questions you cannot answer
some people's love is like a lesson we carry inside us
i carry the lesson of love as a dancing memory
        of picking flowers in concrete fields
no one can see what grows inside you
my love will fill the gaps in time
        after you have gone
no flowers are left to blow in the wind

Conduction

such is the delight
   when a meeting orchestrates itself
   at a random bar
you get to smile
at the blonde you want to see more of
its much more a delight
   when its at a punk bar
       and she smiles back
a little soul music in the background
  saying "what's going on?"
and just like that - off we go flirting
      she makes it easy for me
to make her smile and laugh some more
  she even drinks a porter like me
next time doll just call
we don't have to leave it to the city
       to orchestrate our meetings

Nostalgia is Ink

i find myself in the same sunny bars
at all hours   cafes like Virginia
where tats on girls cling like skin tight clothes
the order of the day is
whores dressed like waitresses
prancing around serving beers and food
                          to small time criminals
   denizens of the scene like me
we live this nostalgia in places built before our time a
lifestyle where we frequent bohemian skills
seduce ourselves along with the ladies
each time we frequent Virginia's
each time a different girl with a different message
      the end game is the same
  we both are just looking for a fuck
a way to remember we are euphoric
         some drugs bind us
  a way to prime the pump
manic streams with energetic themes
   lead to more of the same

Sounds of Video Crack

roller girls, ink and strippers
i knew i was in over my head
when i ordered a Malibu and rum
   a wave of the hand - coke
that was night one of an ink bender
   night two
a little stogie and Pabst
   skin, fishnets and ink
nothing more for the debauchery
red lips and jesus loves porn stars
   hop   hop   bump is the beat
mixtures manic words
   it's just the mayo
     tall slender curves
it's just fresch and the dirty whores
   swinging for this kat
a little pin up pose
   when the beat goes punk
who can forget the fun
of a debaucherous bender
   smiles are like candy grins
with a side of skin
your ink and tits are divine
   chain smoking the pipe over
black and white tiles of mighty Blue Ribbon
   obey   obey
untitled strands

as i twirl golden strands
   through my taunt hands
it's the red light of midnight

    golden punk locks
        tender kisses
as i touch my skin along the curve of her back
i'll turn my fingers on their side
    subtle erotica
        is delicious

Strange Sex Act Painting

   the belltown red walls with red tiled bar
   translucent black bar glass top
a highbrow selection   punk staff
     rock n roll music
shaking the booty to cat scratch fever
she poured me another drink
i smiled though she was not that cute
 it was just the pose that looked so sexy
               we are overdue
  for sunshine and gorgeous dolls
     ripe and bound
  to the strange cold spring
in a time of climate change
            the sun makes it better
as the subculture may be the mainstream
      the sun brings the skin and ink

The Finite Infinity

sitting through a set
  do i have time or no?
  either way boys
we are going to believe
these Italian dreams are worth the time
our captain put in
     for us is infinity
but for you it's finite
     this path

Wicked Delicious

life ring pier 70, Seattle
  or so they say
the day after lily and the wicked delicious shoot
i still feel a little dirty and a bit aroused
  but am excited and high from the day
elevator pitches land warm fuzzy memories
dancing dolls with tan skin   inked bodies
  it's so nice to hear a real piano in the bar
tap my toe to a melancholy hue
  the bar is glass and back lit green with envy
for the bartender in all black with pink nails
  it's just past eight but feels like midnight
the piano plays a slow version of blues
i drink scotch whiskey   thinking
lily is a little nymph
  playful, joyous, mysterious
full of erotic emotion
  the sensual nature of an inked doll
dancing on my hotel bed with clean white sheets
beautiful just beautiful

An Infamous Return to Bohemian Artistry

sitting on a bench i wrote Manic Rose City from
    so many manic inspirational words
The Fresch Klesch back home in the 'hood
    which unleashed the infamous debauchery
at once the same which drew me here
    sent me away
  the nostalgia smell of bohemian artists
    mixed with suits and debutantes
i can taste it as i stare at the corner
  where my beloved Torrefazione shared
  the early beginnings of Manic Rose City
all the nights of debauchery
 on the north end where i used to stand for hours
in the dark cold bitter winter nights
    trying to capture the light
it's a bloody dog park now
  the ever lasting hum
    of eternal manic energy
the rhythm of my rose city
in Jameson Square, salivating for a drink
  listening to the drunkenness
    in that orange glow
  which is still so full of life for me
the laugh of lovers on a bench near me
  the howl of a dog in distress
   after an ambulance rides by
all full of color and noise
the rhythm of my rose city
  two streetcars in opposite union
rolling electricity in the orange hum
a glass of Jamesons neat in the cold night

Magic Nostalgia

in the darkness of the garden remembering
   so much and dreaming of more
          beer and cigarettes
      on a rainy portland day
  nostalgia beyond repose
for things i know so intimately and love
it's such a long moment to impact your dreams
with visions of the prettiest pussy in portland
  a taste of sweetness
knowing the sultry nature of a woman
  words can accomplish the most amazing response
wet panties
       like a rainy summer day
in this beautiful city
soggy sopping mess of hot stickiness
   in the darkness of my garden

A Smash & Grab Affair

delicious   sensual   erotic
  my three favorite things that drive
  my soul to define my art
the underbelly of life is a seedy mess
        riffraff and debauchery
that crosses the line of indecent to organized crime
i'm brooding over a pint and fag
thinking that to get caught in that underbelly
would taint the pureness of
    a sexual fresch klesch
brooding because
i am an intense punk in my approach
seeking approval without caring what you think
brooding because
i want something i cannot have
i am not willing to change for it
   yet like a fly to a flame
i bump up against it
   without yielding to the heat
brooding because
i know there is no stopping my desire
no room for me to accept
        the underbelly
will it taint me before i get out . . .
    obviously a smash and grab affair is in order
        a sweet taste before i go

My Vibe is Jazz

my vibe is cool like miles on the sax
   leading us on an extended version of nocturnal blues
in the smoke filled room he could feel my soul
        as it took bloom
        as the beautiful betty sent her dreams
mixing in my conscious stream
   pen to paper   late nights
are always spent in jazz bars
   kissing my blues as we drink the dark away
her eyes fall on me to sing
      a song of quick paced stepping tunes
         as the beautiful betty lingers
a sensual note so soft
as the sax fills the space between us
among deep smoke filled breaths
   the rest of the kats feel our tune
      kick the temp up again
they go 'til its last call   then some
   she lays her hand on mine to say let's go!
        we side step our way
        into a midnight street
damp with a moist mist our spirits high
we make our way through the park blocks
back to her one room hall as the night fades
this beautiful betty
            lay satiated naked

The Song of You

there is only joy in the song of you
   we sing in the cold mornings
i can remember how a touch lit the passionate flame
together we could feel ecstasy
   oh how i wish this coke had some whiskey in it
something   maybe
something would be at rest
   all these manic streams coalesce
one thought would be you
   in all the memories of my mind
the joy i know is only self taught
   it feels nothing like the warmth of you
soft brush strokes on clean canvas
   the vibrant acrylics
i dreamed you on that sleepy corner
like i dreamed of the vibrant acrylics on canvas
      it was that painting
which reminded me of all my love for you
     yet it was that corner
the reminders of your simple words
perchance on some random fashion day
   i find myself very far away
              in a Harvard bar
  watching the likes of you
all the colors happen to walk up
   to the stool beside me

Short Steps of Babble

the short steps are prime times two
  as infant giggles her way down the side walk
      first steps are tentative
  in the midst of the bustle of urban design
ever so flowing are her words
  a constant babbling stream of consonant sounds
              that is Emily

Red, Gold and Blonde

sickly sycophants here we go
   up ever winding roads paved in gold
      rusted on the outside
         hollow on the inside
welcome to the rich woman's world of
             pantomime whispers
can you feel it too?
   the cling of nothingness
               ever so inclined
we witness all the blondes
doing that which leads to nothing
     quixotic and the like
i find silver to be a more savory color than any other
the road is red
     the sky is often black in day
          no high yellow moon
       to light the way
this lonely wandering nature is
a vibrant roller coaster of characters and stories
   sung in an induced haze of ecstatic joy

Universal Vibrational Energy

orange three lines
   white on a black background
a simple image and moniker to remember
powerful mind games i play
give me all i desire
   just as powerful is this acceptance
               of who i am
    the swagger in it
it's like a devilish laughter in the day time hours
where orchestrating a meeting with a lover
     leads me into a stylist realm
   controlling people like chess pieces
       i send the vibe to an entropic universe
vibrational energy takes care of the rest
it's a sling shot effect around the moon
   all the women i meet bounce around me
many a time or two
      like time weighted balls of magnetic attraction
we average our existence
to love just one
when all is what i seek to fulfill
        in a life spent to pleasure
     all the women i meet

Inherent Mania

walking from Chinatown during pre-new year
celebrate my city by the bay
  i find myself in north beach then little Italy
this is more my vibe in a very bustling San Francisco
    i grew up just south of here
how different it is to come back as a cognizant adult
  i find i walk the streets like Kerouac
        such a manic city
  this crazy hectic energy makes me wonder
if all large cities are inherently like this
the amplified energy is conducive to my artistry
all the places i go
  are conducive to who i am
everyone loves the outpouring of energy
i am the center for me
        a little intoxicating
i know a moment in time
this entropic universe sends us on and on
like ping pong balls on an expansive journey
   down a never ending road in the high desert
sitting here on Telegraph Hill at XOX Truffles where a
French lady serves more than a cappuccino
  all this place needs is a little more color
          some artist friends
   i would consider it divine

Jean-Claude's Truffles

"end Scotland" reads the white sign on a red brick wall
   the number twenty three is on the middle tan door
below as the rain falls without
   relent in a city known for the fog
i love how i am served by the French
        in an Italian neighborhood
  on Greenwich and Columbus
i thanked Jean-Claude for the Truffles
  and trekked onward in the rain

Hop Scotch Canvas

quick hops on a plane are like playing hop scotch
    a dame in every port as they say
for us who love all the women we can
hop scotch is a simple game of two steps forward
two feet planted side by side
  two steps forward   onward we go
women are temporary islands   stay
for a night or two then off to explore   next
  the road snakes forward like a drunk
playing bumper cars on a bowling alley
  only the lights of passing cars
weave a myriad scream of modern art
standing here on the bridge
i see red lines in one direction, white in the other
        the canvas unfolds colors
   as the subtle shift
is movement in opposite directions
      people at a pace
    where sheep become lemmings

Catch and Release Theory

waiting in an airport like LAX
i am reminded of the skirt i chased and never caught
    how fun the idle frustration
        to chase the super elite
who cared only for her posh shoes
this type of gal a fishing trip for me
a means of entertainment to pass the time
    'til the manic episode ends
 i always operate under the strategy
    of catch and release
an evening or two of pure sexual delight
  to see if she screams
            as my artist lovers do
 because a creative burgeoning soul knows
energy dictates basic activities
   art, poetry, sex   mania
being bohemian is very basic in comparison
 to the posh socialite i am staring at
cannot look at me here in this open social setting
but when i meet her at the Whiskey or MoMo's
    it was quite different
she herself was trolling for someone
    different just like me
someone to satisfy her with touch
   thinking only of her needs
here in LAX she cannot even look at me
    i know she screams as loud as the rest
where her fifth orgasm cascades down her body
   her toes curl from the pleasure
yes it is like this every where i go
  with every gal i meet

it is not an ego thing i confess
   she will remember my touch as the best
i am a bohemian artist whose pulse is to express
the red line streaks out across the horizon
        as the sun sets to my right
     its the sulphate particles
which give it the crimson color of death
  a sunset is more the brilliance of life
there is still a tinge of daylight scattering along
the horizon   black above,
       the silver of blue below
   saying goodbye to my day
its just a glimmer like tossing a dime
   to the myriad of punks
       who line the portland streets

Everyone Needs a Bohemian

on a day capped with lectures and boredom
i sit over my Jamesons and Newcastle
    for a bit of verse before i retire
this bar offers the same fodder as any other
maybe the class of clientele is a bit elevated
   everyone interacts the same when drunk
flirty free subject matter
     good for a few laughs
i wonder if the story ends with passionate cries
are architects less in touch with orgasms?
   there certainly are no lonely gals at the end
of the bar like you find in my portland dive bars
here it seems they come with high class losers
      to pass the time away
   you spinsters without the sacred O
i make them nervous sitting here drinking
    writing and watching
yes fellas, i can touch the O with words
     she knows it from my look
hoity toity hoes are the same where ever you go
they are less experienced here in Denver
     with so few bohemians around

Barfly's Words and Sex

can i write a non-sexual
    non-bar poem?   she asked
why?   i respond
   diversity is a good thing she says
have you read my political poems?
   no - well why do you read
         about sex and bars?
   because i am curious
exactly, me too!
   plus the subject matter is prevalent
in my beloved rose city
   she smiles a flirty smile
       winks at me - exactly!

Futbol Politicos

a couple of accented Englishmen
   talk of who ruined futbol
  in a random Denver bar
was it Leeds United or the Italians?
  rubbish they explain
   it was Real Madrid and the center back
no, it was the English you fools
  who could never play the game they invented
everyone else has flair

Just Words

sitting here watching a square teacher
   read my poetry
it is a comical interpretation
      of what she is thinking
pervert   psycho   nuts
wow – how does he do that?
   i don't believe him
      no-way!

The #44 line to the Village

oh that would be the ultimate
   dark   sultry   erotic
like spice from a warm climate
   like burnt orange on black skirts
in the light of dark locks with orange wings
 i can smell spice
      the crisply warm June air
laughter with dark milky lime
    always hands moving
        ever so sensual she flirts
with herself,   her friend   and for me
   oh her spice is an ultimate
       this vibrant warm climate
a rose city bus to my village

Punk Dating

define single these days
   she is the interesting one at that table
everyone is just listening
dude, she's not even paying attention to you
   pretty boy
that's the longest neat shot of whiskey i have ever
drank
one lone male rides the escalator up to nowhere
mostly just hot air and carbon dioxide
occasionally soft conversations over
   red wine and candle light glasses
   on top of brown hair and the white color
   outside a black sweater

Best in Show

i remember now who said i was best in show
i cannot remember why
i remember how good she tasted
later that night after we drank all those beers
    she rode me like a wild stallion in the open field
              for hours and a day
       'til some part of us wept
a tiny thimble of blood
    a bakers dozen or two is what she told her
friends that friday over mixed drinks
        in mixed company
the males refused to believe it was possible
always wondering how a man can do so much
    the ladies just smiled an envious smile
for her choice in men ended impeccably
          in so many sacred O's
when asked who and how?
    she would only answer he was a poet

Perfection

i am a sucker for a British accent
 must be something about the perceived class
maybe in this case it's because she is a brunette
once you've had one you can never go back
 my history says this is only partially true
at least i have a preference
like a cappuccino versus a latte
    or a joint to a pipe

Flapper Roots

in the village having coffee
   a new set of characters to watch and chronicle
it's beyond the borders in this tiny place
   where community is supremely celebrated
and the thinker toys with three little girls
   dancing on a yellow wall
my colors are everywhere
   surrounding the contrast
      of red and white brick
Fat City is served only for breakfast and lunch
but it's been here for all time
   or at least as long as the village
it's roots are in the early twenties
   definitely my time for roaring fun
having a cafe` is being at the nexus of the universe
    the center with multiple roads
a dual four-way stop designed to slow everyone down
    it's an older generation here
       they do things differently

dirty old man

a young model of mine once said
she looked forward to me when i was old
i would be a fun dirty old man
   chasing after skirt
   being a crazy artist
i have not seen her for some time but wonder
   if she thought of me as a sex fiend
my bohemian artistry lends itself to sex and mania,
     the two go hand in hand
i explore sexuality not to find love
    rather to explore the creative ways
         to pleasure a woman
mania fuels the sex drive
     dissipates the uselessness
   of mixed energy states
as does creating art or going for a walk

i like Parades

look at all the pretty people who walk and talk
        as they prance on by
like models on a runway with nowhere to go
   such idle wealth can clearly be used for
    something better than the perceived nobility of this
modern posh dress code
as an original punk i find all this conformity
   to be a little distasteful
Do you have a unique soul?
   when you dress, speak and act
         the same as the fool next to you
        is there a group soul you all
           take turns using
i admit all the beautiful young socialites
   are fun to chase after
     on occasion you can
catch one who appears
no more attached to their posh code than you or i
    i dare say she has a soul
to those who leave a distaste behind
   they lack a depth of personality
ironically they all taste the same
        cry with pleasure when they cum
   this is why i chase them all
to taste the pleasure that is skin to skin

Inked Barstools

a nice refresher to be able to stop off
for a couple of pints
some stimulating conversation
with a punk chick all inked up
she was a few sheets to the wind
    unable to remember my name
she had been to the Yamhill Pub though
so i gave her my book to remind her
  i quoted her Emily Dickinson – twice –
to illustrate we all should strive
  to be nobody in a public eye
we find ourselves on a pedestal in a bog
surrounded by a mass of boring sheep
  Brenda was her name
she carried her eyes on her elbows
  so she could see behind herself
      black ink on skin
  maybe i will see you at the Yamhill
we can write another Pub Rant
  show those polite motherfuckers
what it's like to be punk and drunk in my Rose City

Skin Season is not Boot Season

'tis the season for flip flops and short skirts
god i love this city
   with it's flirtatious population of betties
each one is primed and ready to be pumped
   pheromones pheromones everywhere
scented chemical signatures that you cannot get at home
scented chemical signatures that you cannot get at home

Flames are Blue

the world of the poet is neither triste or joyful
   but rather the person is tragic or accomplished
in the way they interact with the world
a subtle difference that distinguishes the choices
the person excludes blame
   for others choices – what many call
                    their lot in life

whores hats and painted skin

the morning after two gorgeous dolls
        laid my energy bare
  i see a blue moon on pale grey sky
in the early hours before my eyes open
i awaken to blue sky and sunshine
   portland summer sun
warm and delightful
    like a night of painted skin
    on French whores with bohemian hats
    fishnet legs for miles
French whores are open vessels of sexuality
i cannot contrast the photography any different
after having shot them in the pearl
   if i am this brilliant for the work i do
   to French whores with bohemian hats
i capture an inked skin beauty
open vessels of sexuality
   who display luscious lips aplenty
   with perfect erect nipples
      ripe for pleasure
how does it translate for these words i write on paper,
bound in books that sell
         in retail stores for twelve dollars
can brilliance be transferable across media?

Per Capita Skin

kinky dolls aplenty
   in this grey filled sky town
they call the rose city
a small town metropolis with more strip clubs per
capita than anywhere else in the U.S.
   we sell tits, ass and the labia skin
oh beautiful rose city
                     in dive bars
filled with hipsters, punks and posh socialites
we mix drinks and drugs like they are free
                     the dolls are
the sex is a positive action
to drown the depressing grey days
they outpace the rain
   leaving us all a bit wanton
something to bring us a little joy
              sex and sunshine
no guilt, just be free when i call

This Show is Inked

on a full morning of golden leaf paths
   the sun is warm instead of crisp
tonight i debut a set of nude photographs
in a medium as much sacrilege as it is mixed
are digital photographs on par with my black and white film?
       or is it a mixed media print?
only the devotees will tell me
   guaranteed is the night of debauchery
tales to tell you of tomorrow
   first, i am sitting with a cappuccino
dreaming about cigarettes and the list of sexy models
         who are coming tonight
  in the village with the old codgers
who laugh at the misfortunes of the radical punks
the new age excessive smokers who fuck on mind
numbing drugs like vicodin or oxycontin
  very different from the times of shady back alley
streets and heroin chic
   as these new aids are doctor prescribed
the village coffee shop
laughing codgers, artistic baristas, trendy sex kittens
on a fall morning warmed by the sun
a night of inked dolls and debauchery   naked
  where in a village the Fall colors
are golden and the pace
  is less hectic than a manic city
i am sitting at a nexus point enjoying my caffeine and cigarettes

some moments are definitive before they happen some
are definitive because of the outcome
the circumstances in between
   i like to participate in
good or bad, right or wrong
it was not clear to me the type of definite moment
it was after our day shoot, sex and whiskey session
   until saturday night   my latest show
where i debuted my digital color nudes
   i included a book of contact sheets
one sexy dolls pointed out your contacts that day
there was more intimacy in yours than all the others
   that day, in all its sexual erotic glory
our intimate relations the catalyst of change
   definitive, yes   because at the pinnacle
  all the actions, interactions and intimacy
cascaded away   left on film

Punk's Guide to Dating

the life of a single man is quite fundamental
they each have a differing structure and means of
finding satisfaction
    the punk's guide to dating
step one is women are like juggling balls
  you should have as many in the air
so at anytime you want
      there is one in the hand
step two is to orchestrate a meeting
  so you happen to run into a doll
      you are interested in
  it is good to do this periodically
with all the dolls you have in the air
  so they remember why their hearts flutter
      when they are around you
step three is to be a character she remembers
with a smile and a tingle between her legs
a punk always does his own thing
  defines his terms to take what he wants
      when he needs it
hence the quintessential three steps are foundation to
a punk's desire to date
for a punk dating is a pastime
    of drinking, smoking and chasing skirt
the punk dream of idolized debauchery

drinking, smoking, cursing delicious barfly

a delicious read comes
  with a fuck and a night cap
this is what the poet says of his hipster groupies
      who frolic around him
  after a poetic demonstration of his lover prowess
    drinking, smoking, cursing
  a barfly at noon on tuesday
the dirty dolls love the daftness even more
  they usually want to touch the pleasure
      they do not care for me
but rather want to fuck the character i portray
  a delicious read just adds to the story
a legend in my own mind
  is a comical way to say i have talent
despite the artistic establishment
  i am infamous in the scene
everywhere i look my work has quality
    substance and panache
greatness transcends all my faults
  the imagery is crisp   iconoclastic
mixed with taboo and debauchery
    everyone loves to hate
the shock and awe approach

Be a Character

i create what i like from the things i see
        be a cool character
  a kat so you can love all the ladies
drinking polygamy porter as fast as i can
in a salt lake city where last call is at 8:30
    anywhere else the fun hasn't even begun
the word polygamy makes me chuckle
      because literally you cannot
                        have just one
  isn't that the rebel rousing doctrine
      we artistic hepcats live by
one woman now 'til you find the next and so on
    excess is best when accomplished
              in reckless abandon
abandon only when self aware
      the consequence
    may hurt otherwise

Naked Betties

after a long weekend with the betties
   naked and delicious to photograph
i find the early morning flight to the right coast
         a bit bizarre and somewhat surreal
all this time to sit and think
   the naked dolls are fresh memories to recount
all the delicious skin
     areola mingle with lips,
  labia and the O face
all models delight in the fresch klesch

ala carte

the dating revolution
among the young urbane populace
   it should be called the hookup
or one night stand revolution
when you get right down to the frisky nature of it
get you a little something you can take home
   as many side dishes as one can take
no extra cost and she may even call you
         the next day for a little more
   these relations are like combustible chemical
reactions with a low activation energy
just add alcohol and mix two people wanting a fuck
   instant reaction with pleasure
the possibility
a slight hangover in the morning

Delicious Luminous Doll

delicious is the word
  that makes the dolls feel sexy
luminous is the word which best describes
the post coital euphoria they feel
after i have paced their orgasms to a baker's dozen
we met at the bettie ford clinic on twelfth
        had a few cocktails
she looked more like bettie page
  we laughed, shared stories and flirted shamelessly
she laid her hand on my arm
slowly pulled it away lingering skin to skin
i knew it was time to go
  the evening of pleasuring her at hand
out the lounge we plunged
    into still cold April air
down twelfth we sauntered
  drinking in each other as we touched,
hugged and began the aggressive
    accent of flirtation
          the first kiss skin to skin
two blocks down twelfth at the light
    slide my palm to the small of her back
pulled her close   smiled
  she looked in the eye
our lips brushed and the first real trickle
   of passion sparked the car horns
la la OC

less than two days in the OC
  i find i forgot what the cold rain
    of Portland does to you

Huntington Beach is as laid back as it comes
   no-thing like the wilds of LA
the dolls are blonde
the boys are surfers
   everyone smokes pot
what is there not to love
   sunny, warm and a fresh ocean breeze
without the deep ocean smell
        you find up north

Slim Sexy

the fool said,
   i want to be slim and sexy
like all the people i see
i said,
   i want to be a character everyone remembers
     he chuckled as he looked at me
          you are welcome in the OC
la la land is where hepcats are immortalized
     the fools are chased after
at least it's sunny and warm here
    as they say

Prolific Ecstatic Joy

prolific poetry comes from
turmoil pain and   ecstatic joy
   i am lucky to capture the words
as they stream out in an unending audible whoosh
                                  of artistic chaos
   one beer, two beers more - shots
excess is all the same to me
   if you have the time for
sex in an hour
     then all night
will certainly be better
   make way for the mania

Verbose Projections

the rattle and clink of words
   as they hit frozen air
leaves the verbose idealist
   with only cynicism
nothing left on his feet but
   worn out leather shoes
      with holes on the bottom
i am not the man i want to be
   nor the man you want for me
all these variations in self
   tried on like new shoes that never fit
'til you settle for a pair that
   don't make you too uncomfortable
walk out to find yourself
   lost as a man you never wanted to be

Entropy Kisses

scandalous floating eyes on clown heads
   dancing golden bears
this continuous beat
      strewn of diabolical entropy
luscious lips and pantomime kisses
   little whispers in the air
the scent of scandal
      is this LA, NY or London?
i can never tell when you are near
   these altered states are not well defined
entropy always eats your mind

on that note

watching these two lesbians in love
    can only leave me to smile
you gals are so obvious
though i do not remember what it is like
    i can imagine a giddy feeling
in a love song for an inked doll

Due in stores 2/14/11,

A Love Song for an Inked Doll

by Lucas Klesch

Published by Sunshine Ink

Words of Praise for Lucas Klesch's first poetry book entitled Manic Rose City and first published by Sunshine Ink in 2006.

The Danger
"With cool phrases like 'Brutal Blues' and 'Leaves of Industry,' Manic Rose City evokes imagery like Bob Dylan's in Blonde on Blonde."

"I love the abstract phrasing, disco lemonade, vigilante art, etc. Those are the kinds of phrases that really kick a reader in the nuts, makes 'em think a little in different ways, and opens up ideas and possibilities."

Juan Valdez
"The work, I see and read as lyrics to songs like Steely Dan's hopped up on a Jazzy Rock style!"

Available for purchase at Amazon, Barnes and Noble and other fine bookstores everywhere.

Manic Rose City is a roller coaster ride fun house look at the ups and downs of an artist in the rose city, Portland Oregon. It's a world of denizens and hipster characters, each having a distinguishing name for amusement and notoriety. Manic Rose City is the emotional story spoken in vivid Technicolor of the lyrical nature of living an artist's life. It encompasses all the denizen characters who occupy the life and nightlife of this vibrant rose city. Rich with culture, a strong artists colony, and an independent identity, these poems explore all the important themes of life through an emotional fabric of hills and valleys. The poetry is always following some undercurrent of energy in this manic city and is rich with vibrant manic artistic living. The Fräsch Klesch guides us to the characters of the rose city in recurring themes of love, lust, joy and sorrow. The poetry in Manic Rose City is ripe with poignant messages of urban living, human decay, and how there is still a magical place where city dwellers live. Artists consider it their playground where voyeurs love to visit. This book illustrates how an artist struggles with his creative energies, yet is hopelessly full of joy and hope for futures yet explored. It is a compelling tale of love, lust and why poets often are found in bars drinking whiskey on your Tuesdays.

ISBN-13: 978-0976856009

www.ingramcontent.com/pod-product-compliance
Lightning Source LLC
Chambersburg PA
CBHW020703300426
44112CB00007B/489